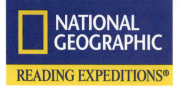

EVERYDAY KIDS THEN AND NOW

EGYPT

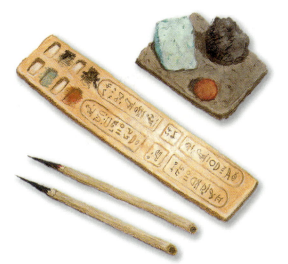

By Jean Bennett

Illustrated by James Bentley

PICTURE CREDITS
3 (top to bottom) © Fergus O'Brien/Getty
Images, © Royalty-Free/Corbis, (border)
© B.S.P.I./Corbis; 6 (map) Mapping Specialists,
Ltd.; 7 (top to bottom) © Sergio Pitamitz/Getty
Images, © David Boyer/National Geographic
Image Collection; 45 (left to right)
© Thomas Hartwell/Corbis, © Reuters/Corbis;
46 (top to bottom) © Bojan Brecelj/Corbis,
© David Copeman/Alamy Images; 48 © John
Lawrence Stone.

Produced through the worldwide resources of
the National Geographic Society, John M. Fahey,
Jr., President and Chief Executive Officer;
Gilbert M. Grosvenor, Chairman of the Board;
Nina D. Hoffman, Executive Vice President and
President, Books and Education Publishing
Group.

**PREPARED BY NATIONAL GEOGRAPHIC
SCHOOL PUBLISHING**
Ericka Markman, Senior Vice President and
President, Children's Books and Education
Publishing Group; Steve Mico, Senior Vice
President, Publisher, Editorial Director; Francis
Downey, Executive Editor; Richard Easby,
Editorial Manager; Bea Jackson, Director of
Design; Cindy Olson, Art Director; Margaret
Sidlosky, Director of Illustrations; Matt
Wascavage, Manager of Publishing Services;
Lisa Pergolizzi, Sean Philpotts, Production
Managers, Ted Tucker, Production Specialist.

MANUFACTURING AND QUALITY CONTROL
Christopher A. Liedel, Chief Financial Officer;
Phillip L. Schlosser, Director; Clifton M. Brown,
Manager.

EDITORS
Barbara Seeber, Mary Anne Wengel

BOOK DEVELOPMENT
Morrison BookWorks LLC

BOOK DESIGN
Steven Curtis Design

ART DIRECTION
Dan Banks, Project Design Company

Published by the National Geographic Society
1145 17th Street, N.W.
Washington, D.C. 20036-4688

ISBN: 0-7922-5817-7

2010 2009 2008 2007 2006
1 2 3 4 5 6 7 8 9 10 11 12 13 14 15

Contents

THEN

Katep the Scribe

NOW

Sahar and the Treasures of Time

Katep and Sahar

The two stories in this book are connected. One story takes place long ago and the other takes place in the present. The same object becomes important in each story for different reasons. Each main character, in the stories has an adventure that occurs in the same place, but thousands of years apart.

Katep the Scribe

This story is set in ancient Egypt over 3,000 years ago. Katep is a farmer's son, but he dreams of becoming a scribe. Katep knows that scribes do important work. They keep records for the pharaoh, Egypt's ruler. For Katep's dream to come true, he will have to travel far from home.

NOW

Sahar and the Treasures of Time

Sahar lives in modern Egypt. When she and her brother visit an ancient tomb, it turns into a day of amazing adventure. Sahar finds a tool that belonged to an ancient scribe. It has the scribe's name, Katep, on it. But Sahar learns that a tomb robber wants it for himself.

Egypt

Egypt is a country that lies on two continents. Most of Egypt is located in northeastern Africa, but Egypt's Sinai Peninsula is a part of the continent of Asia. People have been living in Egypt for over 6,000 years.

Most of Egypt is desert. Almost everyone who lives in Egypt lives along the Nile River. This is because the land around the river is very rich and fertile. People call the Nile River the "River of Life."

The Desert Egypt is part of the Sahara Desert, making the climate mostly hot and dry. The land is sandy and rocky, which means that plants don't grow very well.

Egypt: The Facts

- Size: 386,600 square miles
- Population: 76,100,000 people
- Longest river: The Nile River
- Capital city: Cairo
- Major language: Arabic

The Nile River The river runs through the desert. The water allows plants to grow along the river banks. Egyptians farm the land along the river. Without the river it would have been hard to make a civilization here.

Katep
the Scribe

CHAPTER 1

A Boy Called Katep

Katep sat under a palm tree. He was watching the scribe, Simut, draw marks on a papyrus roll. Old Simut dipped a reed pen into black ink and drew symbols. He was counting the livestock.

Katep waited until Simut had finished. Then he said, "Simut, may I speak with you?"

"What is it, young one?"

Katep spoke quickly before he lost his courage. "I would give all the fish in the Nile River to be able to write as you do."

Simut smiled. "How old are you, Katep?"

"My mother says the Nile has flooded eight times since I was born."

"Eight years old—a good age to start." Simut stroked his chin. "It takes many years of study to become a scribe," he warned. "And you would have to live far away from here, in Thebes."

Katep hadn't thought of leaving his family! He stayed silent for a time. Then he said firmly, "It would be a great honor to be a student."

Simut thought for a moment. Then he spoke. "The sons of farmers do not usually become scribes. But I have no son to help me with my work. I shall speak with your father today."

"Thank you," said Katep. Then he looked at Simut's writing again. He knew that it was about his family's farm. "Why do you count the animals?" he asked.

"I need to know how many cattle a farmer has. Then I can figure out the number of animals he must give to the god Amun-Re," Simut explained. "This is the tax that every farmer must pay."

Katep had heard his father complain about taxes. He worked hard to raise his animals. Then he was ordered to give some of them away. Scribes also came to measure his fields. They would say how much of his harvest must

go to feed the pharaoh's army and workers. Katep kept quiet about his father's objections.

Katep helped his older brothers herd the cattle. He hoped his parents would not object to his leaving because of the farmwork. With four older brothers and three sisters, Katep thought his parents already had enough help.

It was dusk when Katep and his brothers returned home. Katep washed his hands and entered the dining room. Simut was there with his family. Katep's brothers had changed into clean kilts. His sisters wore their best dresses and jewelry.

His father clapped his hands. "Let us eat well. Tonight we have good news for young Katep. In two days, he will leave with Simut to begin a new life as a scribe."

Katep grinned as his brothers slapped him on the shoulder. His youngest sister kissed his cheek. His mother smiled at him, but Katep saw sadness in her eyes.

Katep's father gave thanks to the gods for their food. Then the family helped themselves to the fresh grapes, watermelon, and figs on the table. Katep was too excited to be hungry. He nibbled on some steamed fish and vegetables to please his mother.

After the meal Katep's eldest sister brought out her lute. She began to pluck the strings. His younger sisters joined in with reed pipes. Later,

Katep climbed a staircase to the flat roof of their mud-brick home. This was where he and his brothers slept. They enjoyed the cool night breeze. He gazed at the sky, wondering what his future would be like. He settled down under the cloth canopy with his brothers and stayed awake for a long time.

CHAPTER 2

Katep Leaves Home

It was time for Katep to leave. He felt sad about leaving his family. But he was also excited about the journey ahead. His mother hugged him and slipped a necklace of beads over his head. "To protect and guide you," she whispered.

His father thanked Simut for his kindness. Then he took Katep's hand. "May the gods give you wisdom and keep you safe, my son."

Katep and Simut walked along a narrow track between the fields of golden grain.

At the banks of the Nile, a boat waited for them. They settled themselves on board and the boatman steered onto the wide river. The sail filled with the morning breeze. As they sailed along, Katep watched farmers working the rich black soil that the floodwaters left behind each year. A man lowered a **shadoof** into the river. When a weight on the end of the pole was released, the pole lifted up with the full bucket. He watched lotus flowers and papyrus plants sway in the marshes along the edge of the Nile. Simut pointed to an ibis digging its long black beak into the soil. It looked like a scribe dipping his brush into a pot of ink.

"A good omen," Simut said. "Scribes draw the ibis to represent our god Thoth. Thoth is the god of knowledge."

The breeze carried them farther along the Nile. That night, they stopped at a small village. Katep fell asleep listening to frogs croaking.

By midmorning the next day, their boat arrived at a large town. "Welcome to Thebes," said Simut with a smile.

----

shadoof (shah-DOOF) – a bucket attached to a pole

He guided Katep up stone steps. They led to a wharf where people were buying and selling food and spices. Simut and Katep loaded their things onto donkeys. They trotted past six huge statues. On either side were two giant **obelisks.** "This is the entrance to the temple of Luxor," said Simut.

"The statues all look alike," said Katep.

---

obelisk (AH-buh-lisk) – a four-sided pillar with a pyramid shape at the top

"They were created in the likeness of our master," answered Simut. "The great pharaoh, Ramses II."

Katep gazed at the towering walls of the Luxor Temple. "Does he live in there?"

Simut shook his head. "That place is a temple. It is where people pray to the god Amun-Re and his family."

They left the busy city and followed an inland road.

"Our journey will be over when we reach Karnak Temple," said Simut.

Their donkeys plodded on.

"Is that Karnak Temple?" Katep asked. He pointed to a group of many tall obelisks.

Simut nodded. "It was also built to honor the gods, he said."

Now that they had arrived, Katep felt anxious. "Where is the school for scribes?"

"We go around the temple grounds and enter through a far door," answered Simut. "The school and the students' house are behind the main buildings."

They dismounted and walked along a passage of statues in the shape of kneeling rams. Simut showed Katep the courtyards. They had grand carved figures. Simut pointed out an oblong shape with painted signs. "That is the pharaoh's **cartouche,** his name," he said. "You will learn to write the words of Ramses II on temple walls and papyrus. They will be preserved forever."

---

cartouche (kar-TOOSH) – an oval or oblong figure enclosing an important person's name

Katep looked anxious. "What happens if I make a mistake?"

"Don't worry," Simut smiled. "First you will practice on broken pieces of pottery."

Beyond the temple buildings, Simut led Katep into a schoolroom.

Several boys were sitting cross-legged on the floor. They were watching a teacher explain measurement. The width of four fingers equaled a palm, and seven palms equaled a cubit, the length of a forearm.

Simut introduced Katep. "This is Master Qenna. He will teach you how to figure out the size of farmers' crops," he said. "As a scribe, you will work out the taxes that farmers must give to the gods."

Katep bowed. He wondered how he would ever learn such important things.

"I expect excellent work from all of my students," Master Qenna said firmly.

Simut gave Katep a small leather bag with a drawstring top. "Here is your scribe's equipment," he said. Inside the bag Katep found a wooden

palette, reed pens, and cakes of dried inks.
There was also a small bowl for water to wet
the inks.

Master Qenna dismissed the class. He
ordered an older boy, Teti, to take Katep to the
students' house. Katep ate a little bread and
honey. Then he rolled out his sleeping mat on
the roof, alongside the other boys.

CHAPTER 3

The Schoolroom

In the weeks that followed, Katep studied so much his head ached. He practiced drawing **hieroglyphs** again and again. He learned that each hieroglyph was a picture of a real object. Each picture stood for a different sound, word, or idea.

He sat beside Teti, who showed him how to mix his dried inks with water. With a shaking hand, Katep wrote his own name carefully on a piece of pottery.

"Not good enough!" snapped Master Qenna. He made Katep write his name again and again. At last he said, "That will do."

Katep did well at counting, saying the tables out loud with the other boys. One morning

---

hieroglyph – a symbol or picture that represents a sound, word, or idea in a form of writing called hieroglyphics

Master Qenna was called away from the schoolroom. He instructed the boys to practice their tables until he returned.

Instead, Teti pulled a board game from his bag. "We already know our tables," he said to Katep. "Let's play a game of senet."

Teti placed game pieces beside the board. "You throw first," he said. He handed Katep four flat sticks with marks on one side.

Katep threw his sticks and counted his score. He placed a game piece on one of the squares on the board. The boys concentrated on the game. They both wanted to win.

Suddenly, a shadow fell over the board. A hand gripped Katep's shoulder. Teti scrambled to his feet while Katep was dragged upright.

"Foolish boys!" bellowed Master Qenna. "You must learn to be obedient."

Their punishment was harsh. For weeks, they rose before sunrise. They cut papyrus from the banks of the Nile River. They slit the stalks of the plants into strips. Then, they soaked them in water. Each evening after their lessons, they laid the papyrus strips out in two layers in a crisscross pattern. Then they beat them hard to bind the fibers into sheets.

Katep tried hard to gain Master Qenna's approval. Now he always paid attention in class. His teacher watched him closely, but never offered a word of praise.

Sometimes Katep crossed the Nile with Simut to the tombs of the **nobles.** Simut was preparing his own tomb there. Katep helped him decorate it with hieroglyphs. Brilliant paintings showed Simut counting cattle in the great estate of the god Amun-Re. In other paintings, he was kneeling in prayer with his wife.

"We need to prepare well for our lives after death," said Simut. "The prayers we write on the walls will help us to speak in the next life."

Carefully Katep copied the sacred texts in red ink on the walls. Simut corrected any mistakes he made in black.

---

noble – high-level member of society who worked for the government

CHAPTER 4

Katep the Hero

Every year, the Nile River burst its banks. It flowed over the land. This water made the soil very rich and fertile for crops. At the beginning of the flood, the students were given a holiday. It was for the grand Opet Festival. Everyone looked forward to the festival, when crowds gathered to honor the gods. Temple officials even gave people loaves of bread and jars full of things to drink.

Katep felt excited as he watched singers and dancers marching in a procession. Priests were carrying four ceremonial boats from Karnak Temple to the river. Each boat held a shrine with a statue of a god inside. One of the statues was of the god Amun-Re.

He noticed Master Qenna marching proudly among temple priests. They were slowly moving toward the Nile. The model boats would be placed on elaborate barges and carried upstream. Katep followed the jostling crowd to the river's edge.

As the people pushed forward, Katep heard a shout. He looked along the riverbank and saw a man fall into the swirling waters. Katep ran toward him. Quickly, he grabbed a rope lying near a boat. He flung it to the man. It was Master Qenna!

The teacher grasped the rope. He began to pull himself toward the riverbank. Katep quickly

wrapped his end of the rope around a stake on the bank.

He helped Master Qenna onto dry ground where he lay gasping for breath. In a hoarse voice the teacher said, "I'm forever in your debt, young Katep."

Master Qenna took Katep's arm for support. They returned to Karnak Temple and together they gave thanks to the gods for saving the teacher's life.

After the festival, it was back to studying for Katep and his friends. The months rolled by and Katep worked hard. Most nights he was so tired that he fell asleep as soon as he lay down. But sometimes he stayed awake, thinking of his family and his home.

One morning Simut instructed him to collect his things for a river journey.

"It is time for us to leave. We must count the

farmers' cattle and work out the taxes for the god Amun-Re," he explained.

"Will . . . will we . . ." Katep stumbled on the words. He was afraid to ask what was in his heart.

Simut understood. "Of course," he smiled. "We will visit your family."

Katep beamed with joy.

Sahar
and the Treasures of Time

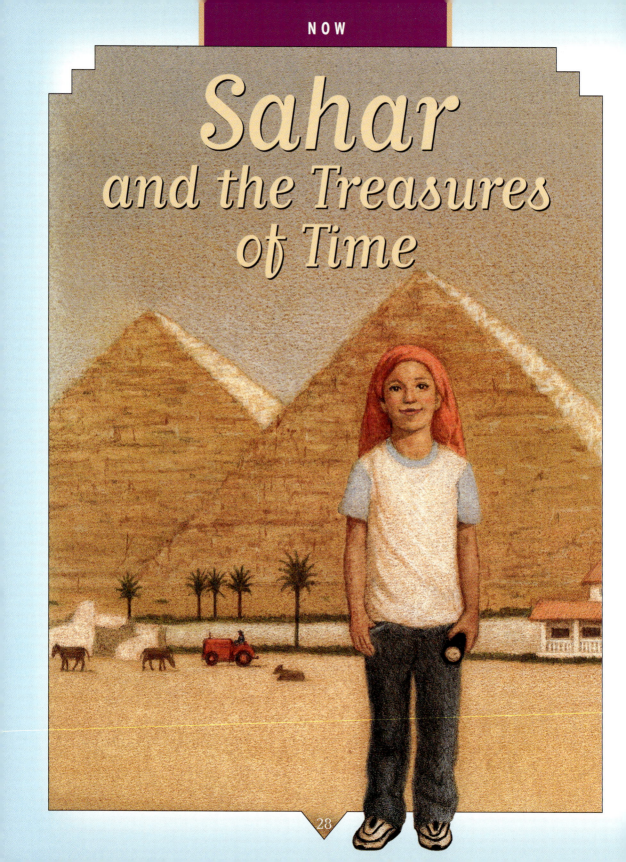

CHAPTER 1

School Holidays

Sahar stood beside the family's cow in the courtyard of her house. She placed a pail under the cow. Then she sat on a low stool and started milking.

The school holidays had started, and she thought about what she wanted to do. She could hardly wait until tomorrow for the Moulid Festival in Luxor. It was a big celebration that honored a saint. But even more exciting to her was a visit to the ancient burial tombs on the edge of the Nile River. She released the cow and carried the full milk container home to the kitchen.

"*Shokran.* Thank you," her mother said. There was little furniture in the room. There were only a few wooden chairs, a blanket-covered couch, and a television set in the corner.

Sahar rolled up her sleeves. She began to knead some dough into flat rounds of bread. Then she mashed cooked beans and spices for breakfast.

Her brother, Ahmed, came in from feeding the geese. Their father, Husam, followed him. He had been fishing in the Nile. He had caught two fish.

The family sat down at the table. Sahar glanced across at her brother. "Ahmed," she said, "can I visit the tombs of the nobles with you over the holidays?"

Ahmed was an archaeology student. He was preserving the murals, or wall paintings in the tombs. Sahar loved to hear him talk about his work. She especially liked the ancient stories that the murals showed.

He smiled at her excitement. "Since we visited the pyramids last year you have really taken an interest in Ancient Egypt," he said. "So, is today soon enough for you?"

Before Sahar could reply, her father spoke. "Is that wise?" he asked. "You said there's been trouble with tomb robbers in the area."

"We'll be fine," Ahmed reassured him. "There are guards always on patrol now."

Sahar leaped to her feet. "I'll pack our lunch," she said, to halt any more objections.

"We'll need flashlights too." Ahmed pushed his chair back from the table. "I'll get the donkeys ready."

Sahar gathered water, bread, fruit, and flashlights. Ahmed saddled up their donkeys. Sahar packed their things in the saddlebags.

"Take care," Sahar's mother said, as the pair waved good-bye.

Ahmed and Sahar headed toward the burial tombs of the nobles. They bumped along a dirt road, through farms and fields of sugarcane.

Soon they reached a village with aged, mud-brick buildings. Sunlight reflected from the whitewashed walls.

"This is Qurna (GUR–na)," said Ahmed. "There are underground tombs here. But many of them have been looted since ancient times."

Sahar looked around the village. "It looks as though it's been here forever," she said.

Raised voices from an alley drew their attention. Sahar saw several men in long **galabias** quarrelling. Suddenly, a short man with a red shirt broke away from the group. He ran from the alley. In his haste, he bumped into the side of Sahar's donkey, near the saddlebags. The startled animal kicked up its hind legs. It tossed the man aside. Then it bolted, with Sahar clinging to its neck.

The man hurried away. Ahmed rushed after Sahar. Sahar's donkey came to a pile of rubble and stopped abruptly. Sahar let go of the donkey's neck and fell to the ground.

----

galabia (guh-LAH-bee-uh) – a loose garment with full sleeves and a hood

Ahmed halted beside her and dismounted. "Are you all right?" he asked anxiously. Sahar lay on the ground, groaning.

"Of course I'm not," Sahar snapped. "I've broken every bone in my body." Ahmed helped her to stand. She brushed dust from her clothes.

"I think it's your pride that hurts most," Ahmed said, laughing. "You looked like one of those rodeo riders on American television."

"Be quiet," Sahar said, punching his arm. "Anyway, what happened back there?"

"Another man from the alley tried to catch the man who ran away. He shouted out that he'd better pay back the money he owed or else."

Sahar looked over her shoulder to see if there was any sign of the men now. She saw no one.

CHAPTER 2

Simut and Katep

Sahar and Ahmed walked to the rocky area near the tombs. Stone and mud-brick walls separated the tombs' entrances.

"We can't see the tomb I'm working on because it isn't finished," said Ahmed, tying their donkeys to a post. "But I'll show you a tomb that Egyptians and Americans cleaned and repaired together. It belonged to Simut the scribe."

A guard who knew Ahmed unlocked the entrance to the tomb for them.

"Pull the door shut when you leave," the guard said. "I'll be patrolling for a while." He grumbled, "Lots of robberies lately."

Sahar felt in her donkey's bags for their flashlights. Her fingers closed on something long and flat. Puzzled, she drew out a wooden board. It had some symbols carved on the front.

"What's this?" she asked.

"A scribe's palette," Ahmed said, with awe. "It's very old. And those symbols are hieroglyphs." He looked at them carefully. "Oh, that says KATEP."

"Katep," repeated Sahar. "Maybe that's who the palette belonged to."

"But how did it get into your bag?" asked Ahmed.

Suddenly Sahar understood. "That man must have dropped this into my bag by accident when he bumped into my donkey," she said. "He's a tomb robber!"

Ahmed nodded. "Maybe he tried to sell it to the men in the alley, or exchange it for his debt."

"What should we do with it now?"

"We'll take it with us for safekeeping," Ahmed said. "I'll give it to the authorities."

Sahar flicked on her flashlight. Ahmed led the way into a dark chamber. "Welcome to the tomb of Simut," he said. "Scribe and chief counter of cattle for the god Amun-Re. He died more than three thousand years ago."

Ahmed shone his flashlight around the walls. He pointed to a mural of a man and woman dressed in white. "Here's Simut and his wife," he said. Another mural showed a man standing beside cattle. Ahmed pointed to the wall. "His title and name are written in front of him."

Below Simut was a picture of a young man herding oxen. Sahar looked at the hieroglyphs above the cattle. "What do they mean?"

Ahmed read the inscription. "Cattle of the Opet Festival."

"What's the Opet Festival?"

"It's a bit like the Moulid Festival that we're going to tomorrow," Ahmed explained. "There was a grand parade to take ceremonial boats from Karnak Temple to Luxor Temple."

Sahar smiled at the similarity. "We follow

boats that are carried through the grounds of Luxor Temple. And we make a grand parade around the town."

They moved around the tomb. Their flashlights flickered over the paintings of Simut's life and stopped on one from his death. It showed Simut's funeral and his river journey into the next life.

He showed Sahar another scene. "Here's a young scribe carrying his equipment. He's following a priest at Simut's funeral."

"Maybe that's Katep," she murmured.

Ahmed led the way into a second chamber. At the very back of the room was a shrine with the remains of four statues.

Sahar's head began to ache. "I need some fresh air," she said. "I'm going outside."

"I'll follow you in a minute," said Ahmed.

As Sahar came into the daylight, she saw a man pull a brick out of the courtyard wall. He was taking something from the hole.

"Hey!" she yelled, recognizing the robber. Startled, he turned to glance at her. Then he ran toward his waiting donkey with a parcel in his hand.

Sahar hurried back inside the tomb and called for Ahmed. By the time he reached her, the robber was long gone. They looked at the place in the wall where the brick had been. All that remained was a small cake of dried color.

"Scribe's ink. Probably from Katep's palette," Ahmed said. "The robber must sort through the rubble after people dig it up from the tombs."

"And he's hidden some things to sell later," Sahar added. "We'll never know all of the things that he's stolen."

"At least I know what he looks like," said Ahmed. "If I see him around the tombs, I'll have him arrested."

Sahar sighed. "Well, it's been an exciting day." She smiled at her brother. "Thanks for letting me see Simut's tomb."

"Time to go home." Ahmed pulled the tomb door shut. The lock clicked. "We'll need a good night's sleep for the Moulid Festival tomorrow."

CHAPTER 3

The Moulid Festival

ahar and her family walked along a dusty track through fields of vegetables. As they reached the riverbank, her father pointed to a small boat with a white, triangular sail.

"We'll go to Luxor by **felucca**," he said. "It won't take long."

As Ahmed cast off, wind filled the sail. They glided past palm trees. Sahar watched a boy standing in a small boat. He was beating the water with a stick to drive fish into a net. Farther along, children played in the river. Long-horned cows grazed near the water's edge. A farmer raised a shadoof from the Nile on the end of a long pole. Huge cruise ships crowded the river. Graceful feluccas moved among them.

----

felucca – a small boat with a white, triangular sail

"We're here," said Ahmed as he steered the felucca alongside a jetty.

Boats of all sizes were anchored along the bank at Luxor. Tourists spilled from the ships and mingled with local people. Guards kept a close watch on all the activity.

"Ahlan wa sahlan. Welcome!" a street seller called out to them.

Sahar's father led them to a line of horse-drawn carriages. "Are you going to hire a *caleche?"* she asked, pointing to the vehicles. "We can take part in the parade too!"

Her father smiled and chose a horse harnessed to a brightly painted carriage. Sahar climbed up front with the driver. The others seated themselves in the carriage. Feathers on the horse's head nodded up and down as it trotted off.

They rode past buildings with balconies overhanging the street. They saw people riding bicycles, and an elderly woman with a crate of squawking hens balanced on her head. Men sat in streetside cafés. They sipped strong coffee.

Sahar waved to a group of her school friends. Some were in long robes. Others wore western clothes. They were all chattering happily. Beyond them, she glimpsed a familiar figure in a red shirt.

"Ahmed!" she called. "It's the robber."

Ahmed and Sahar leapt from the caleche before their parents could stop them. They dodged decorated floats and grumbling camels. They darted between honking cars. Ahmed reached the man first and gripped both of his

arms tight. Some guards pushed through the crowd toward them.

Sahar took a parcel from the man's hand. She unwrapped it and held out a broken piece of pottery. It had symbols painted on it.

"What is it?" she asked.

"It's an ostracon (AHS-trah-kahn)," Ahmed said. "Scribes used to practice their writing on old pieces of pottery."

"This was probably Katep's," said Sahar. "I bet the robber found it with the palette."

She looked at the robber. "I suppose you were going to sell this, and Katep's palette, too," she said. The man hung his head.

Ahmed told the guards what had happened at the tombs and showed them the ostracon. The guards arrested the robber and led him away.

"You did well, Sahar," said Ahmed.

"We both did," Sahar smiled. "Now we can really enjoy the festival." Sahar and Ahmed joined in the slow-moving procession. They clapped and chanted with the huge crowd and swayed to the beat of the drums.

Egypt Then and Now

Tombs Then Ancient Egyptians built tombs for their dead. They wrapped dead people in cloth. The cloth helped to preserve the body. The wrapped bodies were called mummies. Mummies were placed in tombs.

Tombs Now People in Egypt don't make mummies or build tombs anymore. Today, the tombs of ancient Egyptians help us understand their culture. Archeologists are people who study ancient people. They study the contents of tombs to learn about ancient Egyptians.

Writing Then In ancient Egypt, people used a type of writing called hieroglyphs. Each glyph, or picture symbol, stood for a word, idea, or sound. Very few people in ancient Egypt could write.

خفف السرعة
الآن
**REDUCE SPEED
NOW**

Writing Now In modern Egypt, some signs still use pictures. But people usually write in Arabic, and sometimes in English. These languages use alphabets. Each letter stands for a sound. Today, most people in Egypt know how to write.

Write a Compare-and-Contrast Essay

Think about the characters in the stories you read. How is your life similar to and different from theirs?

- Choose one of the characters, Katep or Sahar.

- Copy the Venn diagram below into your notebook.

- Use the diagram to show how your life is similar to and different from the character you chose.

- Use the example for Katep below to get started.

- Write a one-page compare-and-contrast essay about how your life is similar to and different from the character's life.

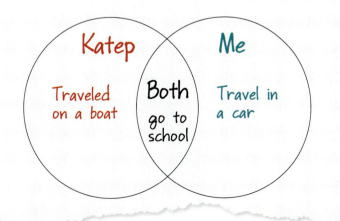

Read More About Egypt

Find and read more books about Egypt. As you read, think about these questions. They will help you understand more about this topic.

- What was the climate of ancient Egypt?

- How did the climate of ancient Egypt affect the people who lived there?

- Why was the Nile River important to the people of Egypt?

- What were some of the customs of the people of ancient Egypt?

SUGGESTED READING
Reading Expeditions
Civilizations Past to Present: Egypt

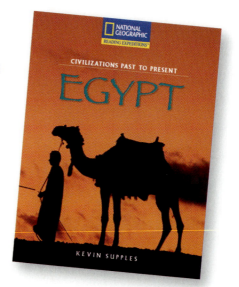